Stock I

Beginners: Marijuana

Stocks - How to Get Rich

With The Only Asset

Producing Financial

Returns as Fast as

Cryptocurrency

By Stephen Satoshi

Contents

Financial Disclaimer:
I am not a financial advisor, this is not financial advice. This is not an investment guide nor investment advice. I am not recommending you buy any of the stocks listed here. Any form of investment or trading is liable to lose you money.

Medical Disclaimer

This book is not intended as a substitute for the medical advice of physicians. The reader should regularly consult a physician in matters relating to his/her health and particularly with respect to any symptoms that may require diagnosis or medical attention. Any recommendations given in this book are not a substitute for medical advice.

Affiliate Disclaimer:

I too believe in transparency and openness, and so I am disclosing that I've included certain products and links to those products on in this book that I will earn an affiliate commission for any purchases you make. Please note that I have not been given any free products, services or anything else by these companies in exchange for mentioning them in this book.

Accuracy Disclaimer:

All prices and market capitalizations are correct at the time of writing. Price and market cap information is sourced from official sources. All information in this eBook was derived from official sources where possible. Official sources meaning literature that is publicly available, provided by the company or official company website.

Free Bonus!

As a gift to you for downloading this book I'm offering a special bonus. It's a free, exclusive special report detailing 3 microcap coins with huge growth potential in 2018. I guarantee you won't find these discussed in any mainstream cryptocurrency forums or newsletters. These 3 were picked as a result of weeks of research on microcap cryptocurrencies.

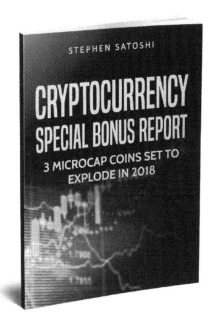

Grab the free report here!

Or go to http://bit.ly/FreeSatoshiReport

Introduction

Outside of cryptocurrency, the marijuana industry in the fastest growing asset class on Earth. In 2017 alone it grew by more than 30%.

That growth is showing no signs of slowing down and legal marijuana is projected to be a near $25 billion industry in the US alone by 2020. Between the US and Canadian stock exchanges, there are now over 220 securities which can broadly be described as "marijuana stocks".

And that's even with the US federal government listing Marijuana as a schedule 1 drug. That's in the same category as cocaine and methamphetamine. It may also surprise you to discover that despite this rapid boom, there is still only 1 single federally approved growing facility in the entire United States.

However, a number of factors in the coming year indicate that this is all about to change.

You see, 29 states now allow legal use of marijuana for recreational purposes, medical purposes, or both.

And the ball is already rolling for further state by state legalization.

64% of US citizens now support legalizing the drug nationwide, that's compared to just 25% when the same question was asked in 1995. 70% of citizens are opposed to a federal marijuana crackdown, according to a poll conducted by Vice. Among younger people, that number is now at a staggeringly high 94%. It goes without saying that the average American's view of marijuana has drastically changed in the past 20 years.

Nationwide legalization of medical marijuana in the USA is now a matter of *when* not if.

And that's not even considering Canada's move to legalize recreational marijuana. The country has already legalized medical marijuana nationwide, and this next move could have an even bigger effect on the market as a whole once the bill passes, which is currently projected to be in the summer of 2018. Canada has its own list of marijuana stocks which offer a tremendous money making opportunity.

No wonder it's been dubbed "the green rush".

Marijuana doesn't just have great investment potential, there are a huge number of economic and social benefits as well. The positive effects are already being seen in early adopter states like Colorado. The first state to approve recreational marijuana use, saw a 30% year-on-year rise in legal sales since 2012. This resulted in $200 million extra dollars in the state's bottom line from tax revenue. Colorado is using this money for good, as much of the money is being reinvested into educational programs and drug-abuse initiatives.

These are exciting times ahead for marijuana both on a medical and recreational level. And there are so many different ways to profit from this. These aren't just limited to the growers and distributors of the plant. Everything from real estate to biotech to a company that manufacturers tiny plastic tubes will be covered in this book. We'll also be doing an analysis of 12 different highlighted marijuana stocks and their different business models.

I hope you enjoy this book and that the information inside proves valuable to you.

Thanks,
Stephen

So just *how* legal is marijuana these days?

One of the more confusing elements of the booming marijuana industry is the legality of it all. In the USA, while marijuana is still illegal at a federal level, different types of marijuana availability is decided on a state by state basis.

As previously noted, recreational marijuana, available to anyone over the age of 21 in the same vein as alcohol is currently legal in 8 states. Medical marijuana, available to anyone over the age of 21 with a doctor's prescription, is legal in 29 states. Now here's where it gets confusing with medical marijuana is being illegal at a federal level. So technically, possessing marijuana is still a federal crime in these states, even if you have a medical marijuana card. This leads to some confusing legislature such as jobs being able to fire employees for off-the-clock marijuana use. Landlords can also evict tenants for marijuana use, even if their state allows it. What we should be concerned with most as an investor is the main law that affects medical marijuana companies. This is the law that means many of these companies cannot get access to full banking and credit due to the federally illegal nature of their business, the law was put into place to prevent drug dealers from laundering money through banks. We'll be going on to discuss how this affects marijuana businesses later on in this book.

Below is a full breakdown of the exact legality of marijuana and cannabinoids on a state-by-state basis.

States That Have Legalized Industrial Hemp Production

- Alabama, Arkansas, California, Colorado, Florida, Georgia, Hawaii, Illinois, Indiana, Kentucky, Maine, Michigan, Minnesota, Mississippi, Montana, Nebraska, Nevada, New Hampshire, North Carolina, North Dakota, Oregon, Pennsylvania, Rhode Island, South Carolina, Tennessee, Utah, Vermont, Virginia, Washington and Wyoming.

States That Have Legalized Hemp Oil/CBD Hemp Oil

- Legal in all fifty states, though CBD Hemp oil is still illegal in Idaho, Indiana, Kansas, Nebraska, South Dakota and West Virginia.

States That Have Legalized Medicinal Marijuana

- Alaska, Arizona, Arkansas, California, Colorado, Connecticut, Delaware, Florida, Hawaii, Illinois, Maine, Maryland, Massachusetts, Michigan, Minnesota, Montana, Nevada, New Hampshire, New Jersey, New Mexico, New York, North Dakota,

Ohio, Oregon, Pennsylvania, Rhode Island, Vermont, Washington, Washington DC and West Virginia.

States That Have Legalized Recreational Use of Marijuana

- Alaska, California, Colorado, Maine, Massachusetts, Nevada, Oregon and Washington.

It is also predicted that a further 5 states: Vermont, New Jersey, Michigan, Oklahoma and Utah - will each legalize adult recreational marijuana by the end of 2018.

Supply and Demand

One obvious, yet often overlooked factor in the marijuana market is the supply and demand of the plant. This has historically been difficult to quantify due to the previous illegality of the drug, and thus a lack of consistent evidence. Many investors naturally assume that legalization across more and more states will lead to increased demand, which is true.

However, something that is also true is that supply is actually outstripping demand. For example, in California, locally grown supplies are up threefold from 2006 to a staggering 13.5 million pounds a year. In the past 2 years, the wholesale price of marijuana has plunged from around $2,100 per pound to $1,600 per pound. This is not only due to increased competition as more and more growers enter the market every year. There is also the technological advancement in growing techniques, which is further lowering wholesale prices. Great for the consumer, but obviously not so great for the growing companies. Until federal nationwide legalization, it is also difficult for these growers to be able to sell their excess harvest to other states due to the different laws in place. Therefore there is no option to take advantage of geographical arbitrage by growing in states with lower land prices, then selling in states with wealthier consumers.

The interesting caveat to this is that the current fear North of the border in Canada, is that supply will not be able to meet demand is nationwide legalization does occur in the summer of 2018 as is expected. Current estimates don't favor producers, and many believe that it will be at least 2 years before they are able to consistently meet the demand for marijuana across the country.

Other estimates are less optimistic and have this figure at nearer 4 years before demand can be met.

Marijuana producers are scrambling to agree on a deal on a state-by-state basis and we are also seeing companies work together in order to try and streamline their processes so they can meet demand.

Marijuana Real Estate

It's not just growers and sellers that are profiting from this "green rush", the real estate market is being turned on its head. As more than 20 states have legalized medical marijuana, as a result, an under reported yet significant part boom is the form of real estate. This being the land that marijuana growers, factories and stores utilize. Even celebrities are getting involved, including former Heavyweight Champion boxer Mike Tyson has just purchased a 40-acre ranch in a remote California which will be dedicated to growing operations, as well as a luxury marijuana resort for cannabis enthusiasts. Tyson plans to use the ranch to provide jobs for military veterans in the local community.

You see, Cannabis sales are higher per square foot than department stores by 5 to 1. Drug stores by 1.5 to 1, and narrowly beating out Whole Foods. In fact, Marijuana sales per square foot are closer to that of

Costco than any other entity. This combined with the numerous red tape and bureaucracy that marijuana businesses face has led to a significant premium in the average price of real estate for a marijuana business versus a conventional business.

For example, in Denver, the marijuana industry pays on average a 50% premium for warehouse buildings. Sometimes this premium can as much as 2 or even 3 times higher than non-marijuana businesses! Colorado is one of the big winners when it comes to the marijuana real estate boom, and over one third of new industrial tenants are now marijuana businesses.

The biggest opportunities to be had is in states that newly legalize medical and recreational marijuana use. For example, states like Michigan and New Jersey both of whom are on the brink of legalization. However, bills can stall, as we have seen in states like Maine. So, therefore, there is a significant element of risk in trying to "jump the gun" and get a head start on the marijuana real estate boom. There is also the issue of zoning laws and the areas that these businesses are allowed to operate in.

One interesting potential development is how federal legalization would impact real estate with regards to interstate transportation. Right now, all legal marijuana sold within that state must be grown in the same state in avoid to not violate federal drug trafficking laws. However, a nationwide legalization would result in this not applying, and thus companies could take advantage of parts of the country with lower land prices. The biggest losers in this scenario would be East Coast producers who traditionally have the highest land prices of all the legal marijuana states.

This isn't the first time real estate has made its mark in an unfamiliar industry. Let's take a look at McDonald's for instance. Not only is McDonald's and its' Golden Arches one of America's most iconic companies, it's also one of the best performing stocks of the last 30 years. Outperforming IBM and Coca-Cola over the same time period. Many investors shun McDonald's for its low-cost, low-brow business model of offering cheap food to the masses. However, what people really overlook is the *business* of McDonald's.

You see, in investment terms, McDonald's is really a real estate company. A large chunk of their annual profits comes from buying land cheaply, then leasing it at higher prices to its franchisees. One of the simplest business models imaginable, but one that has continued to produce profits, hand over foot, for the past 50 years. Founder Ray Kroc was even quoted as saying "We are in the real estate business, not the hamburger business."

And now, the marijuana industry is undergoing a similar phenomenon. Marijuana businesses are prevented from receiving bank loan or mortgages under federal law. Therefore, nearly all marijuana businesses are forced to rent their buildings at a premium. So it is the landlords who are making a killing off of this.

We've even seen support from institutional investors, in January, a little known ETF, the ETFMG Alternative Harvest ETF moved its focus from Latin American real estate to the thriving marijuana industry. The fund made some big plays, including acquiring over 300,000 shares of Turning Point Brands.

Although it should be noted that the majority of Alternative Harvest holdings are in the growing and distribution sector, that doesn't mean more of a real estate based portfolio can't be counted out in the future. After all, their initial focus was on the Latin American real estate market, so the fund managers have previous expertise in that sector.

It's large swings in focus like what we have seen from Alternative Harvest that indicate that the market is undergoing something of a boom. We may well see further emphasis on this sector as we move forward into 2018 and beyond. Needless to say, there is a certain hysteria around marijuana real estate right now, and many investors are clamoring to get their piece of the pie.

Big Tobacco vs. Cannabis Industry

Big Tobacco is one of the main detractors from the medical marijuana industry. This is the same set of companies that vehemently denied for years that tobacco was dangerous to one's health. It was only the result of a multi-state lawsuit that got them to do so. Funnily enough, there were reports of the tobacco industry gearing up for legalized marijuana as far back as the 1970s. There is even a handwritten memo from the President of Philip Morris Tobacco George Weissman stating "While I am opposed to its use, I recognize that it may be legalized in the near future...Thus, with these great auspices, we should be in a position to examine: 1. A potential competition, 2. A possible product, 3. At this time, cooperate with the government." Philip Morris also formally requested marijuana samples from the Department of Justice so they could carry out their own testing.

The more intriguing part of this memo is the section saying "We are in the business of relaxing people who are tense and providing a pick up for people who are bored or depressed. The human needs that our product fills will not go away. **Thus, the only real threat to our business is that society will find other means of satisfying these needs.**" The last sentence is where the cannabis industry comes into play. Will tobacco companies actively try to put a stop to increasing legalization, rather than trying to enter the market themselves? Only time will tell with this one, however, given their history of opposing marijuana, we may well see this in the near future.

The other option is that big tobacco will look to diversify its own interests with investments in marijuana firms. For example, Imperial Brands (formerly known as Imperial Tobacco), one of the largest tobacco corporations, recently added Simon Langelier to its board of directors. Langelier is the chairman of PharmaCielo, a Canadian based manufacturer of cannabis oil extracts and other marijuana based health products. The tobacco industry in the US is declining around 4% year on year, and the companies may look to marijuana to help offset some of these expected drops in revenue. We have already seen of these companies diversify into the growing e-cigarette industry, and it is likely that we will see some small scale ventures into the marijuana market within the next 18-24 months. Whether this will result in direct takeover bids for marijuana firms is unknown, but it's something we can't count out at this stage.

Big Pharma vs. The Marijuana Industry

Legal marijuana's biggest enemy, in terms of a specific industry, is the pharmaceutical industry. Big Pharma has a long documented history of opposing any form of marijuana legalization, especially for companies focusing on the medical benefits of marijuana.

In 2016, a $500,000 donation was made to an organization opposing Arizona's recreational marijuana initiative. Donations of $500,000 to major political candidates are not uncommon at all, but ones of this size to a group fighting a signal issue are very rare. That $500,000 came from Insys Therapeutics, who manufacture Subsys, a powerful and extremely addictive Fentanyl based painkiller, targeted at cancer patients. This donation ended up playing a key part, as Arizona's initiative was defeated by the narrow margin of 51-49.

What makes this even more interesting is that Insys is now developing its own line of synthetic THC based drugs. So to make this abundantly clear, this pharmaceutical company not only donated money to help block legalization of recreational marijuana, it then released its own synthetic alternative. It should be noted that in December 2016, former CEO Michael Babich and six more Insys executives were arrested in an alleged bribery case revolving around pressuring doctors to prescribe Subsys, along with defrauding insurance providers. This was done with the motivation of promoting Subsys as an alternative to traditional painkillers and to try to capture market share.

Then you have the case of the 2014 Community Anti Drug Coalition of America (CADCA), where speakers pleaded against the legalization of marijuana. One of the main sponsors of this program was Purdue Pharma, the company that happens to manufacture Oxycontin.

Over 1,000 deaths per year in the United States result from overdoses from prescribed Oxycontin. This number soars to over 100,000 when we account for a worldwide scale. Abbott Laboratories, the maker of Vicodin, is another large contributor to CADCA. It is estimated that Big Pharma spends upwards of $20 million per year in lobbying anti-marijuana initiatives.

Early estimates have put medical marijuana's competition as having the ability to cost Big Pharma between $4 and 6 billion per year in direct loss of sales. Washington, for example, has seen a decrease in Medicare prescriptions since the legalization of medical marijuana. Phizer, one of the largest drug companies on the planet as produced data showing that medical marijuana could take as much as $500 million out of its bottom line revenue.

Where Big Pharma's motivations lie to clear to see, the issue is a financial one, rather than a moral one. They are fully aware that nationwide legalization would eat into their market share, as customers seek alternatives to mass manufactured chemical drugs. This competition would lead to lower prices, which is the last thing the pharmaceutical industry is interested in.

Therefore it is likely we will be seeing more companies follow the lead on Insys, in manufacturing their own synthetic THC and CBD based drugs, which could bypass federal restrictions and therefore be sold in regular pharmacies across the country, rather than only in specialist cannabis stores. The potential market size for this is huge, as it is now estimated that over 100 million Americans now depends on some form of painkiller on a daily basis. This includes both doctor prescribed medications such as Vicodin or Percocet, as well as street drugs like Heroin. One thing marijuana enthusiasts have long since spoken out against is the possibility that Big Pharma could use its own pockets to corner the market with these synthetic cannabis drugs, as the general population will view them as "safer" due to their presence in regular pharmacies.

It will be interesting to monitor drug developments in the next 18-24 months from this larger pharmaceutical companies, as they seek to get their own share of the ever growing medical marijuana market. I would predict that we will be seeing more and more synthetic cannabis based drug options emerging from the traditional pharmaceutical companies.

Cannabinoids

You may have seen reports of companies who are focused on "cannabis medicine", what these companies do is utilize cannabinoids to create drugs and formulas to treat various diseases.

For those are you who aren't familiar, cannabinoids are the chemical compounds found in the marijuana plant itself. The main ones being THC, the psychoactive compound, which creates the "high" marijuana is known for. The other main compound is CBD, unlike THC, CBD is non-psychoactive, so you can take pure CBD based products and not feel a "high". Because of this distinction, CBD is legal in more states. There are also other compounds such as CBN, CBG and CBC.

There are a number of biotech companies which focus more on the cannabinoid side of things, by developing pharmaceuticals using these compounds as a major or periphery ingredient. The growth of stocks like these is largely dependent on FDA approval for their drugs, and if you've been in biotech for a while, you'll know this is a slow process.

One of the largest players in this market is the UK based GW Pharmaceuticals. Their main cannabis related product is Sativex. A spray that can help alleviate the symptoms of Multiple Sclerosis. Currently, Sativex has regulatory approval in 16 markets, with 12 more pending. Another drug, Epidiolex, aimed at treating child-onset epilepsy is currently in the pending approval stage as well.

Other significant players in the cannabinoid markets are MedReleaf, Tilray and OrganiGram, all three of these companies are based in Canada are produce CBD based drugs which aid treatment of various health ailments. We'll discuss both MedReleaf and OrganiGram in greater depth later on in this book, as both companies have some very exciting prospects up their sleeves.

"Non-Marijuana" Marijuana Stocks

There are a number of companies that you may well be aware of, and may even hold in your portfolio already, which actually have significant ties to the marijuana industry. As such, I have dubbed these "non-marijuana" marijuana stocks due to their primary business being in different industries.

One such example of this is Scott's Miracle-Gro. A long-time leader in the traditional home and garden care market, a market that usually produces slow, steady, unspectacular returns. Scott's has been a long-time favourite among many US households and known for their TV commercials.

However what you may not have known about Scott's is that 11% of their sales are now derived from a subsidiary company, Hawthorne Gardening Co.

Hawthrone focuses its efforts on the medical marijuana industry, and has been steadily acquiring smaller marijuana businesses over the past few years. There additional focus of the business is on the technological side of things, mainly in Hydroponics, which is the act of growing plants in water enriched with minerals and nutrients. In 2017, Hawthorne's sales tripled, and those numbers are projected to continue rising as we move forward.

Even if sentiment completely reverses regarding marijuana and legalization, Scott's can still fall back on its bread and butter business of traditional lawn care, which makes up 89% of the business in total.

The other issue we can look at is the potential for Big Pharma companies to try to acquire some of these cannabis producers as a hedge against their own day-to-day business operations. These companies have very deep pockets, especially compared to even the bigger marijuana firms. We may see some of the pharmaceutical giants make takeover plays for cannabinoid based biotech firms in the next few years.

Marijuana Industry & Red Tape

Now here's where the state legalization vs. Federal legalization issue gets hairy. Because banks have to comply with federal laws regarding issues like money laundering, this directly affects the day to day marijuana business. You see, as a result of this confusing status, many marijuana businesses have zero access to credit. Some can barely get access to more than a basic checking account. This is because it is entirely possible for a bank to be charged with money laundering if they deal with marijuana businesses. Although I should note at this time, there have been zero instances of this. At the time of writing it is estimated that one third of licensed marijuana vendors have been denied a bank account.

There are also no tax breaks for marijuana businesses. In a similar law that was aimed at preventing illegal drug dealers from deducting business expenses, marijuana companies are now feeling the effects. A strange caveat to this is that businesses such as prostitution and contract killing can still claim deductions. I know what you're thinking, and you are correct hitmen can claim business expenses. The ramifications for this are large across the industry, basic business expenses such as rent, advertising, wages and utilities (a big one for the growers) are not allowed to be claimed by owners of marijuana businesses.

Where this hits home on the bottom line is that many marijuana businesses are looking at effective tax rates (the percentage of their *pre-tax* profits) of 70%, as opposed to the much lower 30% for other businesses. In terms of the larger conglomerates, it is estimated that many US businesses pay an effective rate as low as 12.5%. What's worse is that marijuana businesses can be on the hook for federal tax evasion if they don't comply with these laws. We should remember that it was a federal tax evasion charge that ended up bringing down Al Capone's entire empire in the 1930s.

There is hope though, in 2017, a bi-partisan act introduced by Senator Ron Wyden and Senator Rand Paul would allow marijuana businesses to make the standard business tax deductions. However, the bill is currently stuck in committee though, and it may well be years before it is able to be passed and enacted.

What's more is, many of these businesses are forced to operate in cash. This gets even more absurd when you consider that even though marijuana is still illegal at a federal level, due to tax code 280E, which requires drug dealers to report their illicit profits for tax purposes, the IRS collects roughly $3 billion per year from marijuana vendors. This leads to a number of stories where marijuana vendors are having to pay the IRS in cash at their local office. Marijuana is certainly beneficial to the IRS and industry growth would lead to even more revenue down the line. Data shows that legal marijuana could lead a 6 fold increase in federal tax revenue.

Why could this all go wrong?

All investments come with a certain amount of risk, and it's always good to analyze the contrarian view of the situation, so we will do so here. Here are a number of factors that could mean this all ends in disappointment. I should note before we begin this section, that this is all speculation. Thus you should take it with a pinch of salt.

Industry Consolidation

The astounding growth rate for the industry thus far, and the continued predictions of 26% per year for the next 3 years. However this does mean we're yet to see any sort of industry consolidation, many of these smaller companies especially will be absorbed into the larger marijuana conglomerates that will no doubt be formed within the next few years.

On the flipside of this though, investing early in these smaller companies could well lead to big gains if they are bought out, rather than run out of business by these larger firms.

Penny stocks

Many of these smaller marijuana stocks are defined as penny stocks as they trade under $5/share. Therefore they can't be listed on the NASDAQ or New York Stock Exchange. Many of them will list on Over The Counter (OTC) exchanges, which have lower requirements and monitoring standards than the bigger exchanges you'll be more familiar with.

This makes them more liable to misinformation and less than stellar business practices. I would exercise caution to these tiny marijuana based stocks, as like other penny stocks, they are more likely to be manipulated than larger ones.

News flows slower in the OTC world as well, so investors looking for up to date information regarding important metrics like cash flow, may well be left in the dark for a longer period than they are comfortable with.

The other factor is the vast majority of penny stocks are companies with less than solid fundamentals in the first place. Most penny stock companies are losing money every year, which is a big part of their low price. Others do not yet have a working product and are banking on future approval in order to their stock increase price.

When researching these stocks, you will see phrases like "expansion phase" "potential revenue" and "impressive management team" rather than talk of consistent profitability or market share. There will also be a group of people shilling the stock on message boards or in private Discord groups. You'll see phrases like "get on the train", "10X by the end of the month" and other fear of missing out type language. If you've been involved with cryptocurrency at all, you'll see the same patterns and language associated with that market.

Like any penny stock, these microcap marijuana companies should be looked at as a speculative gamble, rather than a long or even short term investment. If we want to look at some historical precedence, let's take a look at 6 nanotechnology companies that were previously listed on OTC market. Nanotechnology was another big boom industry in the mid 2000s, and many investors made speculative plays.

JMAR ($JMAR): Down 100% from its peak

Biophan ($BIPH): -99% from its peak

US Global Nanospace ($USGA): -99% from its peak

Industrial Nanotech ($INTK): -96% from its peak

Natural Nano ($NNAN): -99% from its peak

mPhase ($XDSL): Down -99% from its peak

If you had invested $1,000 in each of these companies, so $6,000 total, you would currently have **15 cents to show for your initial investment.** So if you are not an experienced investor, or you don't have deep pockets, I would urge you to stay well away from these microcap companies for the reasons listed above.

Jeff Sessions

Attorney General Sessions is one of the biggest critics of the marijuana industry. Sessions has been previously quoted as saying "good people don't smoke marijuana" and "My best view is that we don't need to be legalizing marijuana." Needless to say, statements like these don't fill the room with confidence when it comes to the issue of nationwide legalization.

Sessions also strongly believes the gateway drug theory, that many opioid addicts were exposed to the ideas of illegal drugs via marijuana and thus marijuana is the direct cause of their addictions. Despite a large number of academic studies that have long since refuted this theory, Sessions continues to stand by his views.

What is more concerning is that these statements were made, despite increasing amounts of data supporting the medical and social benefits of legalized marijuana. For example, in 2015 there were 20,101 deaths resulting from opioid related overdoses. Contrast this to a grand total of ZERO deaths from marijuana related overdoses. You can't really argue for stronger data than that when it comes to legalization, and yet here is one of the most powerful men in the country using phrases like "historic drug epidemic".

The positive of this is in the form of the President Donald Trump himself. During his campaign, he stated multiple times that he was a supporter of medical marijuana, and said the issue should be decided at the state level. Trump's views on drug legalization are well documented in the past, and he was even quoted in a 1990 Miami Herald interview as stating "We're losing badly the War on Drugs. You have to legalize drugs to win that war. You have to take the profit away from these drug czars."

However, there is a possibility that Sessions could try to override this by repealing the Rohrabacher-Farrr Amendment. Needless to say, the man who said "I reject the idea that America will be a better place if marijuana is sold in every corner store." is going to be one of the largest hurdles to overcome.

Canada backtracking on legalization

For the Canadian stocks talked about in this book, the path appears to be smoother, but that doesn't mean bumps in the road can't happen. Whilst recreational marijuana legalization is scheduled for summer 2018, a lot can happen between now and then. Originally supports had hoped for an announcement for July 1 2018, which happens to be Canada Day, but Prime Minister Trudeau ruled that out in December 2017. Any further delays could lead to decreased industry confidence, which will no doubt have a negative effect on market sentiment and share prices of Canadian based stocks.

Public Sentiment Regarding Legal Marijuana

The sentiment is an overlooked part of analyzing a market. General public opinion is a huge factor in both the short and long-term growth of an industry. Often, short-term price changes are decided mostly on sentiment rather than any fundamental changes with a company or industry. We have seen this multiple times with cryptocurrency and the price volatility associated with that particular industry.

In February 2018, Marijuana Business Daily released their "Marijuana Business Factbook", an almanac of statistics relating to the marijuana industry and its potential growth going forward. The big takeaway is that they have now upgraded their projection from 3x growth to 4x growth by 2021.

The second biggest indicator that we could be poised for solid long-term gains is the public opinion poll carried out in the research. 59% of Americans now favor legalizing marijuana, a number that continues to creep up every year. In addition to this, only 32% of Americans are now fundamentally *opposed* to legal marijuana. Once again, going by age, the younger generation is more fervent in their support.

In total, there have been 5 major opinion polls in the past year alone, and their results all say the exact same thing. The majority of the US population is in favor of legalization, both on a medical and recreational level. One survey, by Quinnipac, solely focused on medical marijuana, and a whopping 94% of respondents supported the idea.

An Analysis of 12 Marijuana Stocks

In this section we take a look at a number of marijuana stocks, the companies behind them, and how they plan to capture their part of the marijuana market. Not all of these are pure play stocks, so not all of their revenue is directly tied to marijuana, but all of worth investigating, to say the least. As always, I am not recommending you buy any of the stocks listed here.

It should be noted that although a number of these are Canadian stocks, some do trade on OTC exchanges in the United States.

Scotts Miracle-Gro ($SMG)

Price at time of writing: $89.13

Probably the most well known of the "marijuana stocks" in this list. We should note off the bat that the marijuana component only makes up around 10% of Scotts total business, but this is an ever growing proportion. We previously mentioned the 2015 purchase of General Hydroponics, which will be a key factor in Scotts expansion into the marijuana sector going forward. General Hydroponics provides both consumer and industry indoor growing solutions, which will be huge if recreational marijuana is legalized on a wider business, and could result in a rise in the company's important to Scotts bottom line..

A dip in price at the beginning of 2018 was to be expected, as the lawncare business that makes up 90% of Scotts revenue is extremely seasonal. As the hydroponic portion of the business grows this will likely even out as the nature of hydroponics make it a seasonproof growing tool. Grow wise, further expansion into other aspects of the marijuana business may well be on the cards, and a company like Scotts has deeper pockets than most, thus would be able to afford any short term losses as a result of growing pains that these new ventures can often cause.

Another area of interest for long term investors would be Scotts extremely strong fundamentals and track record within the sector. The company is now 150 years old and has been a household name for many years before legalized marijuana was on the radar of most Americans.

GW Pharmaceuticals

Price at time of writing: $126.06

The biotech giant from Britain is one of the more well known "marijuana stocks" although unlike many of the others here, they do not participate in the growing or distribution market. GW's usage of marijuana is in the manufacturing of drugs known as cannabinoids, in which marijuana is a key component.

Their current flagship product is Sativex, the first cannabis based treatment to receive FDA approval in the United States. Sativex helps treat the symptoms of Multiple Sclerosis (MS) including pain relief, bladder control and involuntary muscle spasms. The success of Sativex has helped GW rise into the ranks of one of the top performing biotech stocks of the last few years.

GW is now betting big on Epidiolex, a CBD based drug that will help epilepsy sufferers, particular those with child onset epilepsy. In discussions with insurance providers, it is planned that if approval is gained, the drug will be available to over 200 million Americans on their healthcare plans. As previously discussed, developing new drugs can take a long time when you factor in everything from lab development, multiple testing phrases and the huge amount of red tape that comes with trying to get FDA approval.

GW received good news though in December 2017 when they revealed that the FDA had approved their New Drug Application for Epidiolex. This doesn't mean they have the all clear to manufacture and sell the drug yet, but it is certainly a step in the right direction. If the FDA approves the drug in the middle of 2018, the timeline will mean that the drug could be on the market within 3 months.

There is another cannabinoid in GW's pipeline as well, the lesser reported Cannabidivarin (CBDV) which is being developed to help treat epilepsy in adults. There have already been tested on CBDV in treating symptoms of autism in young children. However the development is in the early stages and therefore will have no bottom line impact on GW's revenue this year, and approval by the end of next year is also unlikely.

GW's strong fundamentals have led to some financial analysts labeling it "the most secure marijuana stock". Whilst biotech as an industry operates different to pure marijuana stocks, there may be additional benefits as any federal rulings on recreational marijuana use are unlikely to affect the development of cannabinoid based drugs. Overall, compared to some of the riskier plays here, GW offers the conservative investor an easy entry point into the marijuana market.

Kush Bottles ($KSHB)

Price at time of writing: $5.50

Kush Bottles is a marijuana company, that doesn't actually deal with the growing or handling of the plant at all. The California firm provides and distributes the materials needed to grow marijuana and marijuana products at an industrial level. This includes everything from child-safe packaging, labels, vape pens, cannabis pipes and other paraphernalia. Their flagship product is a plastic tube to safely store a pre-rolled marijuana joint. While this may seem fairly inconsequential, pre-rolled joints are a big feature of legal marijuana that did not exist when it was still illegal. Every marijuana dispensary worth its salt features pre-rolled joints heavily, and being able to capture this part of the market could mean big things for Kush Bottles going forward. Currently, the firm boasts over 4,000 legal marijuana customers, and in a sales presentation July, stated they sold over 1 million of their pre-rolled tubes to dispensaries every month.

The company is still very much in its early stages, with only $18.8 million in recorded revenue in 2017. However, the firm is not up to it neck in debt like many smaller marijuana companies which can be seen as a big positive. In its first 3 years of business, the firm has acquired 3 competitors already in the form of Dank Bottles, CMP Wellness and Roll-Uh-Bowl.

Growing pains will be in line with many other marijuana firms regarding basics like tax deductions and banking regulations.

Cronos Group ($MJN)

Price at time of writing: $9.20CAD

Cronos Group takes a slightly different approach to the industry. Rather than focusing its effects on cultivation or distribution of marijuana, the firm acts as an investment group for Canadian medical marijuana companies. The firm currently owns 3 marijuana companies outright and has partial holdings in 3 more.

Cronos is betting big on the proposed legalization in summer 2018. Legalization would give a boost to all of its companies, and the diversified nature of its investment mean it can withstand additional competition in certain parts of the industry such as growing. Competition is still a concern industry-wide, and short-term effects could be an increase in advertising spend as it fights for market position. However, this should not be a concern for those looking to hold long-term.

Another thing to note is that Cronos and its subsidiaries are not yet profitable, so investors can expect additional share issuances. The amount of shares in play has increased by a factor of 10 within the last 4 years, and with each new issuance comes a devaluing in the current value of shares. In terms of short-term viability, Cronos has a lot of eggs in the legalization basket, so it may be worth holding off on pulling the trigger until that matter is sorted out.

Emerald Health Therapeutics ($EMH)

Price at time of writing: $6.53 CAD

The Canadian pharmaceuticals company, formerly known as T-Bird Health Inc. is another company with more of a focus on the medical marijuana space. The company producers cannabis oils, dried cannabis as well as marijuana based health solutions in capsule form.

The firm is more research based than other medical cannabis producers and makes an effort to identify the most important qualities in each marijuana strain, before isolating those properties and creating new products from them.

Growth towards the end of 2017 was fueled by a purchase of additional growing space and the company was also given a recent upgrade to Tier 1 by the Toronto Stock Exchange. This indicates solid financial reporting practices and generally shows the company is well run.

One additional point of interest with EMH is their adoption of blockchain technology. Blockchain technology is the underlying digital ledger which allows cryptocurrency to function securely among other things. EMH will be using the technology to help develop supply chain and ecommerce solutions in a joint venture with DMG Blockchain Solutions. The venture will be named CannaChain Technologies and as expected, will focus its initial efforts on the legal cannabis industry.

Medical Marijuana Inc. ($MJNA)

Price at time of writing: $0.11

Famous for being the first publicly traded marijuana company in the United States. The stock has been trading for over 4 years, which makes it a grandfather in a space seeing new firms pop up every week. The firm operates in both the marijuana and industrial hemp fields. This includes selling hemp oil, CBD oil and other cannabinoids aiming to treat various health ailments.

Because none of these oils are THC based, MJNA operates more on the legal side of things than other companies. CBD oil, for example, is legal in all 50 states. However, recent FDA rulings may complicate this matter, as the FDA wishes to regulate CBD based products due to them containing miniscule amounts of THC. This continued fight led to share prices tumbling more than 70% in 2017, and there doesn't seem to be much potential good news on the horizon for the company.

The company operates a number of subsidiaries, which has led to small calling it a small scale marijuana ETF. The interesting structure of these companies and exactly how their profitability works is a factor that could lead to investor caution. There is also their large numbers of shares issued (3 billion at time of writing) which may also be a factor in looking elsewhere for solid marijuana investments. As such, MJNA looks at this stage to be a highly speculative play at best, and one probably suited more towards serious investors with much experience in penny stocks.

MedReleaf ($MEDFF)

Price at time of writing: $18.00 CAD

MedReleaf is another Canadian company just spends more of its focus on the medical marijuana side of things. As a manufacturer and producer of cannabis oils and dried cannabis, it targets those holding medical marijuana cards. Their 2017 IPO was North America's largest marijuana IPO yet.

The medical marijuana industry in Canada continues to grow at a rate of 10% per month, that's right, not per year but per month. Cannabis oils are growing even faster than that at a rate of around 16% per month. Oils have a much higher margin than dried cannabis, and therefore MedReleaf is able to grow its earnings at a much higher rate than competitor companies who only focus on the dried plant. The company controls roughly 45% of the cannabis oil market in the country, and with their expanded production facility, this percentage could well go even higher.

This has led the company to post decent financial numbers in the past few years. Although the company is not yet as profitable as others like Canopy and Aphria, it continues to be well run and has not yet diluted shares to raise capital like some of its competitors.

MedReleaf's growth plans include expanding their Bradford production facility to 86,000 square feet. This will allow the company to keep up with the ever increasing demand, especially if the legalized recreational marijuana bill passes this year. Their focus on higher margin products, and positioning to take advantage of any proposed legalization makes MedReleaf a very exciting prospect to watch. Most marijuana companies aren't profitable and are betting on the future rather than the present. MedReleaf is one of the rare exceptions to this rule.

Organigram Holdings ($OGRMF)

Price at time of writing: $3.30

Based in New Brunswick, Organigram is one of only two companies (the other being marijuana giant Canopy Growth) with a license to produce marijuana in the province. Why this is important, is that New Brunswick is the only Canadian province with fully legal recreational marijuana use. This led to an almost 200% increase in the number of patients that Organigram serves, with this total projected to rise further in the next 12 months. All of this comes before nationwide legalization currently scheduled for summer 2018.

With estimated produce levels topping 65,000 kilograms a year, the firm shows that it means business. All this comes from just a single production facility, which Organigram plans to expand in 2018. As well as moving into higher margin strains of marijuana. The company also has a dried cannabis sales arm, although the growth of that element of the business has been slow.

This makes Organigram a prime target for a buyout from one of the larger corporations. With a market cap of $400 million, along with its previous connections and licenses, one of the bigger firms may well be taking a look at Organigram as a way to enter New Brunswick. The company also has an agreement in place to supply Prince Edward Island with 1 million grams a year which will work out in an additional $7-9 million in sales.

Potential problems include the ability to scale their operations that quickly, especially when marijuana companies are in somewhat of an arms race to increase their production yield as fast as possible. Being first to market when the recreational legalization deal is made will be huge, and Organigram is competing against some heavy hitters in this respect. Their current agreements alone though make them well worth checking out.

Update: A February press release noted that OrganiGram had received additional licenses to expand their production facilities. Construction of a new facility with estimated 65,000 kilogram yield per year is now due to begin in April 2018. This is very positive news for the company going forward.

Canopy Growth Corp ($TWNJF)

Price at time of writing: $22.35

Canada's Canopy Growth Corp is a big player which currently holds around a 20% market share.

Canopy has been quick to expand, and last year purchased Mettrum Health in a deal which included 2.4 million square feet of land with the capacity for growing marijuana.

Obviously, the big external factor will be whether Canada passes legal recreational marijuana in the summer of 2018 as is expected. Currently, there don't seem to be too many hurdles in the way, and Prime Minister Justin Trudeau is leading the charge himself. One important factor to note is that the proposed tax rate for the newly legalized marijuana is much lower than any of the state tax rates we have seen in the United States so far. This will allow marijuana to be priced at more competitive rates, and eliminate competition from the black market, which has been a thorn in the side of some states like Washington.

This is combined with the number of Canadian medical marijuana increasing by a staggering rate of almost 10% per month. Canopy's Canadian presence is one of the factors that helped it overtake GW Pharmaceuticals as the world's largest marijuana stock by market cap in November 2017.

Canopy also exports dried marijuana to many European countries that have legalized the drug including the Netherlands.

One factor to watch with Canopy is if the new legislation brings about an influx of competition in the space. While this is to be expected, it remains to be seen what effect this will have on Canopy stock prices going forward. Needless to say though, for the time being, Canopy can safely say it holds the position as King of the Legal Marijuana industry.

General Cannabis Corp ($CANN)

Price at time of writing: $4.12

General Cannabis Corp has a wide range of business including consulting, advisory, marketing, and management services to the marijuana industry. Their holdings include a 3 acre property in Colorado, as well as a branding and marketing firm that targets the marijuana industry.

Their website doesn't really tell you more than that, using terms like "trusted partner" and "turn your dreams into reality." rather than making more concrete statements about what the company can do for potential clients. The homepage also features a stock ticker, and the company Instagram account, which are two facets of business that don't usually appear side by side.

The balance sheets are rather alarming with less than $300,000 in assets and over $4.5 million in liabilities. That ratio alone is frankly terrifying. The company also made a $9 million loss in the past year with just $2 million in gross sales. With numbers like this, it's hard to say just how much of a future the company has, and it obviously cannot continue to make big losses like this. Overall, I can't see much upside for General Cannabis Corp and its investors going forward.

Aphria ($APH)

Price at time of writing: $16.08CAD

Aphria concentrates on providing hydroponic solutions for medical marijuana. The company currently has a partnership with the Canadian government and this is part of the reason the stock tripled in price during 2017. The company currently has around 40,000 patients and a fledgling nationwide distribution system.

Aphria is one stock that defies industry norms in terms of producing positive revenue growth and ending the financial year in the black. Strong fundamentals like this make the stock a promising one to monitor as we go forward. Revenue increased by 62% last year and the last quarter's earnings were also positive. The ability to not only promise a product, but actually deliver on a profitable one, is something that could well indicate strong long term potential.

The company also acquired Broken Coast Cannabis for $230 million (note: this was a largely stock funded deal with only a small fraction coming in cash), which gives them better access to Canada's West Coast. Late January also brought news of the acquisition of Nuuvera in a huge $826 million cash and stock deal. The deal was made with the intention of moving growth beyond the Canadian borders, and international expansion seems to be on the cards. Nuuvera was already working with parties in Germany, Israel and Italy to explore distribution opportunities for newly legalized medical marijuana. The Italian market alone is worth around $9 billion annually and Nuuvera is one of the few foreign companies with a license to export goods to Italy. This aggressive growth strategy is one that may put Aphria into the big leagues in an industry that is consolidating at rapid rates.

February brought news of an international supply chain agreement with Cannabis Wheaton. This will help both companies advance their distribution strategies in order to keep up with the ever increasing demand. This may be bigger news for Wheaton than Aphria in the short term due to the company's smaller size, but working agreements like this show that co-operation on future projects, which may have more benefit to Aphria, is on the cards.

Corbus Pharmaceuticals ($CRBP)

Price at time of writing: $7.05

Corbus is focused strictly on the medical side of the marijuana equation. It's currently betting big on its drug Anabasum. Anabasum aims to treat sclerosis and has done well in initial trials. There are also plans to trial the same drug in relation to Lupus.

After a meteoric rise at the beginning of 2017, with prices soaring over 500% in the first 3 months, the stock began to cool off towards the end of the year. Like most smaller cap companies, Corbus is yet to be profitable. Current cash flow analysis indicates the company has enough money to continue its day-to-day operations into Q4 2019. Although this could be extended with a stock offering.

The obvious concern is whether Corbus is a one trick pony, and as of right now, that's probably a correct assumption to make. If Anabasum doesn't get approved then its back to square one, and with a lack of profitability, that may well be it for Corbus. However, if Anabasum continues to produce positive results and ends up getting FDA approval, then Corbus will move on to bigger and better things, much to the delight of investors.

Marijuana ETFs

At the time of writing, there are 3 approved marijuana ETFs in North America, with two more scheduled for launch in February 2018. For those of you looking for a more low-risk, hands off option for investing in marijuana stocks, one of these ETFs may be exactly what you are looking for. That's before the obvious advantages of ETFs like only paying 1 commission vs. Upwards of 15 commissions if you were to buy the individual stocks.

In December 2017, ETFMG Alternative Harvest ETF became the first ETF to list on a US stock exchange. We have previously mentioned this ETF and discussed how their decision to pivot from Latin American real estate to the marijuana industry may be cause for concern. The move comes with buying popular marijuana stocks such as Canopy, Aurora and GW Pharma.

The price action after the move was heavily in the positive direction, just take a look at this chart from Bloomberg after the decision to buy marijuana stocks occurred.

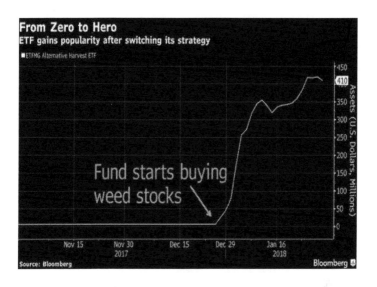

What you may not know about this ETF that's been in the news so much over the past 2 months is that it's Custodian Bancorp is considering dropping the ETF due to its drastic switch in the business model. This move also appears to be based on the uncertain future of federal level marijuana legalization. There is, of course, the probability that if Bancorp does drop the ETF, that another bank will step in and fill its shoes. However, if they cannot find a replacement, the ETF will have to be liquidated.

Switching focus is not necessarily uncommon for an investment group to do, however, it is the complete industry pivot that is something we must examine. As indicated by the graph above, the fund remained relatively flat before the move to marijuana, so their track record in other industries isn't something we can verify. The next 6 months will be interesting and it remains to be seen if they can replicate their initial short term success.

Horizons Marijuana Life Sciences ETF ($HMMJ)

Price at time of writing: $18.76CAD

Launched on the Toronto Stock Exchange in April 2017, this ETF has been one of the top performers since the beginning. Posting gains of over 85% in 2017, although it has experienced some pullback to start 2018.

The fund focuses more on the medical marijuana industry and has a policy of not buying any companies that focus strictly on recreational marijuana in the US or Canada. However, this view is likely to change depending on how quickly legalization occurs in both countries. You can certainly expect investments in recreational marijuana companies if legalization goes through in Canada this year as expected.

The fund holds 30 stocks, which is generally considered a low number for an ETF, and as such your diversification is lower than other ETFs, making it naturally a riskier proposition. Another factor to examine is the proportion of the fund that is held in the top 20 stocks. In the case of HMMJ, the top 10 (not 20) stocks make up over 80% of the fund, which is somewhat concerning for the low-risk investor. The top 4 holdings are naturally the large Canadian medical marijuana companies, namely Canopy Growth Corp, Aurora Cannabis, Aphria and MedReleaf.

Some investors would like to see additional diversification in form of biotech companies and cannabinoid firms, although these companies tend to be in the slower growth rate sphere due to the long process of their drugs receiving approval, and therefore aren't without risk themselves.

HMMJ is certainly the most fundamentally sound marijuana ETF, and with a management fee of 0.75% plus sales tax, it's not an expensive one for the retail investor to get involved with either. If you are looking for a lower-risk way to enter the marijuana market, this could well be it.

Horizon Marijuana Growers ETF ($HMJR)

Price at time of writing: Not yet launched

Another ETF by Horizon, this one focuses on the growing and cultivation part of the industry in particular. This particular ETF consist mainly of small cap companies with upside potential and aims to take advantage of increased demand for marijuana across Canada pending the legalization of recreational marijuana.

One interesting thing to note about this ETF is that 20% of the holdings will be made up of overseas companies, in the first instance, this will be growers from Australia. This could certainly help negate some of the risks that comes with banking on summer 2018 Canadian legalization. The first group of holdings has CANN Group as the largest with 7.24% with its Australian growing company AusCANN making up a slightly lower portion of the fund.

The fund will have a 0.85% management fee. So if you're someone who has huge faith in the demand for growers, then this ETF might be a smart play for a low-risk investor who doesn't want to go in on just one or two individual companies.

Evolve Marijuana ETF ($SEED)

Price at time of writing: Not yet launched

Scheduled for Launch on February 12th 2018, this will be the 4th ETF in North America and will trade on the Toronto Stock Exchange. Evolve Funds Group CEO Raj Lala stated the fund aims to take advantage of "a 60-per-cent compounded annual growth rate in the next few years." It is unclear just which sector of the market the ETF will target, but they have stated they will be investing in both domestic and global marijuana companies. The initial focus will be on the Canadian market, but as legalization gets more traction worldwide, expansion beyond its borders will occur. You can fully expect that the big Canadian companies like Aurora, Canopy and Cronos Group will be among the initial portfolio of holdings.

It has also been stated that the fund will have a management fee of 0.75% per year. Evolve has a strong track record and their first venture into the marijuana market will be an interesting one to monitor. Another Marijuana ETF, run by Redwood Investments is due to launch around the same time period.

Can non-Canadian residents buy Canadian stocks?

As you may have seen, a large number of these stocks are listed on the Toronto Stock Exchange, Canada's largest stock exchange. Some are also listed on US regulated exchanges, which means you can buy them using a local broker, or broker who supports US stocks if you are based outside of the US.

You can also buy Canadian stocks from many online brokers including TD Ameritrade, Schwab and E-Trade, however, there may be higher commissions than US stocks when using these sites. Some of the commissions can be as high as $19 per trade. I advise you to check your broker's rates for Canadian stocks, and it may be easier to call them on the phone than dig through the website looking for rates. At the time of writing, only Schwab uses the same rates for both US and Canadian stocks.

It should be noted that some online brokers do not directly buy Canadian stocks, they instead purchase pink sheets as a proxy for the stock. These pink sheets will have a 1:1 value, but trading volume will be lower than the volume on Canadian exchanges. So this is something to look out for if you are planning on buying or selling large amounts, and I would recommend double checking with your broker before executing any trades.

The other thing to note is if you are using a US broker, you may be looking for a different stock symbol than the ones listed in this book. These symbols will usually be 5 letters long, so make sure to check your particular stock's corresponding US symbol before you accidentally buy shares of the wrong company.

Should I still invest in Marijuana Stocks if I'm fundamentally against marijuana as a drug?

Obviously, some more socially conservative investors will have an opposition to marijuana stocks. Many of these companies will fall into the same category of "sin stocks" as alcohol and tobacco companies, and if you are morally opposed to investing your money in these kinds of companies, that's OK.

On top of that, as we have previously discussed, marijuana still remains illegal at a federal level, and there are a number of ramifications that come alongside this decision. It should be noted, that obviously any publicly traded marijuana stock is conducting its business within the eyes of the law, this goes for small cap stocks traded on OTC exchanges as well as larger cap ones on the NYSE or the Toronto Stock Exchange.

However, that doesn't mean you have to miss out on one of the hottest asset classes in the past 10 years. There are still a number of companies that are focused more on the beneficial side of marijuana. These would be companies more on the biotech side of things that are focused on utilizing marijuana and components like CBD, to cure help diseases.

Firms such as GW Pharmaceuticals fit this bill well, with their epilepsy drug Epidiolex. We should reiterate at this point that CBD, unlike THC, does not have any capacity to alter one's mindstate, so users will not experience a regular marijuana "high". There is also InSys Pharmaceuticals, who we have discussed previously, and their subsidiary company SubSys which is developing a drug called Syndros to assist in helping weight loss associated with chemotherapy.

Other companies like Scotts Miracle Gro have a small marijuana element to their business and as such, can be solid plays without needing to tell your friends you bought a "pot stock". These are just a few options if you wish to get a part of the pie, without committing yourself to a pure marijuana stock and going against your own individual moral code.

Conclusion

Well there we have it, an introduction to the exciting
world of marijuana stocks, and the potential benefits
of investing in them. Like I said before, this market is
projected to triple in size in the next 3 years, and there
is enormous opportunity across many factors of the
industry. From growing to manufacturing and
distribution and real estate, marijuana is going to make
a lot of people rich in the few years.

Like any industry, there is risk involved, and I urge you
to do additional research on top of what you've read in
this book. There are also a number of external factors
to consider, many of these are out of the control of the
companies they will affect, so it would be wise to
monitor any legalization news closely.

Marijuana is still in the early stages as an asset class, so
as such many of these companies should be looked at
as more speculative plays, similar to cryptocurrency in

this respect. Therefore they should not make up a significant portion of your portfolio.

I hope you've enjoyed what you have read in this book, and if you do decide to invest in marijuana stocks, I hope you make a lot of money.

Finally, if you learned something from this book, I'd appreciate it if you left a review on Amazon.

Thanks,
Stephen

Other Books by Stephen Satoshi

Cryptocurrency: Beginners Bible (also available in audio)

Blockchain: Beginners Bible (also available in audio)

Bitcoin: Beginners Bible (also available in audio)

Cryptocurrency: The Ultimate Beginners Guide (contains the
3 above books at a discounted rate - also available in audio)

*Cryptocurrency: Insider Secrets - 12 Exclusive Coins Under $1
with Huge Growth Potential in 2018*

Ethereum: Beginners Bible (also available in audio)

*Cryptocurrency: Top 10 Trading Mistakes Newbies Make -
And How To Avoid Them* (also available in audio)

*Cryptocurrency: 13 More Coins to Watch with 10X Growth
Potential in 2018*

*Cryptocurrency 3.0 - Ultra Fast, Zero Transaction Fee,
Futureproof Coins That Need to be on Your Radar*

*Cryptocurrency: What The World's Best Blockchain Investors
Know - That You Don't*

Made in the USA
Middletown, DE
19 April 2019